Ashton Sixth Form College
Learning Centre
Darnton Road
Ashton-under-Lyne OL6 9RL
Tel: 0161 330 2330

VALENTINO

First Published in Great Britain in 1996
by Thames and Hudson Ltd, London

Copyright © 1996 Editions Assouline

British Library Cataloguing-in-Publication Data

A catalogue record for this book is available from the British Library

ISBN 0-500-01756-5

Printed and bound in Italy

VALENTINO

TEXT BY BERNADINE MORRIS

THAMES AND HUDSON

In the post-World War II years, largely thanks to Christian Dior, Paris regained its position as the centrepoint of international couture. Twice a year the couture showings drew throngs of visitors to the French capital, visitors who not only supported the couture houses, but also brought valuable custom to the grand hotels and smart restaurants. The French government in its turn gave backing to its couturiers through its official body, the Chambre Syndicale de la Couture Parisienne. This organization was responsible for setting the dates for the couture showings and establishing the rules whereby a fashion business could be known as a couture house. The rules included employing a specified number of workers and staging quasi-public showings for six weeks after the introduction of each season's collection. Membership of the Chambre Syndicale was limited to French couture houses – foreigners were not welcome, though they were allowed to come as workers. (This situation would remain even as late as the early 1960s, when the Italian designers Simonetta and Fabiani, a husband-and-wife team who developed separate couture houses, and Roberto Capucci, all of whom had been highly successful in Rome, tried to set up businesses in Paris. Ignored by the establishment, they were forced to retreat.)

after the war, Italy was beginning to develop a reputation for bright, attractive sports clothes. Narrow, calf-length trousers, known as Capri pants, became immensely popular worldwide, as did Italian knits, especially in silk and cashmere. Italian evening dresses and tailored clothes also appealed to both vacationers and store buyers.

Thanks to the many local dressmakers who bought styles in Paris to be copied in their own workrooms, women in Italy were very aware of clothing trends in the French capital. Increasingly, too, they came to recognize what their own fashion requirements were, and began to encourage the development of a domestic market for fashion.

the designer who was in many ways to spearhead that development, Valentino Clemente Ludovico Garavani, was born on 11 May 1932 in Voghera, a small town about midway between Turin and Milan, in the north of Italy. Throughout his childhood he took a keen interest in fashion and in later years became fascinated by painting, sculpture and architecture. A talent for drawing led him in 1949 to enroll in a fashion sketching course at the Santa Marta Institute in Milan. At the same time, he took a Berlitz course in French, revealing a facility for languages which would stand him in good stead when, a year later, he moved to Paris to study at the school run by the Chambre Syndicale. A young man of many interests and passions, he also took dancing lessons and developed a love of French theatre.

Valentino's career got off to a flying start when, as a student, he won a competition for fashion design run by the International Wool Secretariat – Yves Saint Laurent and Karl Lagerfeld were to be winners a few years later. It was a prestigious award which led to a job at the couture house of Jean Dessès.

During this period, when Valentino was learning his craft, he paid a visit to the opera in Barcelona and was struck by the fact that all the costumes onstage were red.

'I realized', he recalls today, 'that after black and white there was no finer colour.' When he began making clothes for his own house, he favoured red above all other colours. It would become as associated with his name as shocking pink had been with Schiaparelli's.

Valentino stayed on as an assistant at Dessès for five years, picking up during that time the couturier's predilection for authoritative drapery and exotic references.

Only a small body of Valentino's work remains from this early Dessès period, consisting of ten sketches which were not produced. He made up the actual garments only in 1991, when they were included in his retrospective show: 'Valentino, Thirty Years of Magic'. The ten styles opened the exhibition and were immediately revealed to be precursors of themes which he would elaborate on later in his career.

The designs show the basic Valentino shape for day and evening as slender, except for a few bouffant dresses of calf or ankle length, as was the style of the early 1950s, before the mini. The surfaces of the slim, long evening dresses are encrusted with jewel embroidery and the narrow shapes are softened by back-flowing chiffon panels or capes. The day dresses are decorated with velvet bands or with a leopard-printed belt matched to an accompanying stole. They are accessorized with stiletto heels and small, forward-thrusting hats.

We can see in this mini-collection the first appearance of

Valentino's red, the prominence of graphic black-and-white embroidery suggesting Meissen china and the black-and-white dress in a shape suggesting a Greek vase. All these foreshadow themes that Valentino would develop in his mature years.

Far more important, however, than any of these details is the unmistakeable sense of elegance and authority. These are in no way the sketches of a tentative student. Rather, it is as if Valentino as a designer emerged fully grown from the head of Zeus. The dresses work and each has a sense of balance and proportion – an astonishing accomplishment for a man in his early twenties.

●

In 1957, Guy Laroche, the chief illustrator at Dessès, decided to open his own salon. Valentino went with him, working at both the design and the business end. Two years later, enriched by this double experience and familiar with the tout-Paris of the fashion world, he made the decision to set up his own fashion house.

In November 1959, with financial help from his father, Valentino presented his first collection of 120 styles in his own salon on the Via Condotti in Rome.

Among the first to be impressed by the young designer was the movie star Elizabeth Taylor, in Rome with Richard Burton for the shooting of *Cleopatra*. She ordered a white dress to wear for the world première of *Spartacus*. Numerous film stars, from Audrey Hepburn and Rita Hayworth to Italians like Monica Vitti, Sophia Loren, Ornella Muti and Claudia Cardinale, to Hollywood's Jessica Lange and current luminary, Sharon Stone, were to follow.

When, early in the 1960s, swinging London caught the world's attention and inexpensive London fashions overshadowed couture,

Valentino was ready to meet the challenge. Within a year, he had introduced his first ready-to-wear collection.

In the same year, 1960, Giancarlo Giammetti, an architecture student, joined the fashion house. He soon became managing director, enabling Valentino to spend more time on the actual designing.

●

In the Autumn collections at the Pitti Palace in Florence in July 1962, Valentino was offered the last hour on the last day of the showing in which to introduce his collection. Foreign buyers, who had heard rumours about the new Italian star, stayed on to watch. Immediately afterwards they raced backstage to place their first orders. Among them were Sydney Gittler and Irene Satz of the famous New York store Ohrbach's, which had been highly successful in promoting line-for-line copies of French couture styles. For these buyers, as for many others, the Paris styles were becoming increasingly expensive and they did not hesitate to turn to Italy. Valentino was a huge discovery for them. The wide press coverage of his shows, plus the Ohrbach connection, soon put his name on a level with the great couture figures.

With this show, he had taken his first step on the road to international recognition. He went on to present his collections around the world and became, not surprisingly, the darling of the Italian press.

But it was his women customers who most spread Valentino's fame. In 1962 Alida Valli was chosen as the most elegant woman at a Venice festival. Two years later Jacqueline Kennedy started to wear his clothes and in 1968 she would choose Valentino as the designer of the dress for her wedding with Aristotle Onassis. She remained a friend of Valentino, wearing his clothes throughout her life. In later years Marisa Berenson and Elsa Peretti were to be his fetish models.

abandoning group shows in the Pitti Palace in Florence in the mid-1960s, Valentino began to introduce his collections in his salon on the Via Gregoriana in Rome. These presentations, scheduled for the last evening of the entire week of shows, became social events in their own right, attracting leading actresses and the wives of politicans and businessmen, all dressed in evening wear.

In addition to the predictable quotient of glamorous, elegant evening dresses, embellished with sequins, feathers and embroideries, there were always some styles guaranteed to attract the attention of the press, including, for example, coloured furs in mauve and pink mink. Any celebrity present was bound to receive attention from the Press.

Valentino's success was almost immediate, and he had soon consolidated his position as a leading couture star, despite the fact that his headquarters were not in Paris, but in Rome. He was not alone in this, of course. Other couture houses in the Italian capital included the Fontana sisters, Princess Irene Galitzine, Maria Antonelli and Emilio Schubert, all of whom occasionally made an impact on the international scene. But the best of these – Simonetta, Fabiani and Capucci – had been demoralized by their disastrous attempt to challenge the French on their own ground.

In the 1960s, Valentino produced many styles that reverberate in the history of fashion. It was a turbulent decade, representing the growth of a counterculture that saw elegant clothes as an irrelevance. But Valentino consistently incorporated details from the world's cultural heritage, from the ancient Egyptian and classic Roman cultures to the paintings of Klimt and Schiele. Echoes of Art Nouveau and Pop Art also gave breadth to his collections. With his combination of art elements plus an imaginative reworking of traditional couture themes, he gave his clothes a sense of history as well as immediacy. His continued use of black combined with white was widely popular and his animal prints, including leopard, zebra and giraffe markings, were timeless in their appeal.

In a period when the chemise made the unfitted waistline the touchstone of contemporary clothes, Valentino chose to retain femininity in his designs by the use of fragile fabrics with elaborate surface embroideries. Feather and fur borders provided the obligatory accents of luxury.

●

I n January 1970, Valentino opened his Spring/Summer collection with a bombshell. Over the last decade skirt lengths had risen until it seemed they could go no higher. Valentino dropped them to mid-calf length. Though it would take a few seasons for this new length to be accepted, everyone agreed that he had made a strong case for a new seriousness in fashion.

At this time Valentino was thirty-eight years old and at the height of his powers. With Saint Laurent, he was considered to be the bearer of elegance and modernity. At last, Italian couture could stand proudly alongside Parisian.

For a few years, Italy could boast a first lady, the attractive and stylish Vittoria Leone. She was hailed as a boon to Italian fashion and occupied a front-row seat at Valentino's shows. He also made the clothes she took with her on a state visit to the United States, garments which received high praise from Pia Soli, fashion critic for *Il Tempo*, in Rome. 'The First Lady's wardrobe is splendid,' she wrote. 'It's the best expression of what Italy is able to create when it comes to fashion, an art that until twenty years ago was the exclusive prerogative of France.'

anticipating the growth of ready-to-wear, Valentino opened shops in New York, Geneva, Lausanne, London and even in the French capital itself. In 1975 he was one of the first to introduce his ready-to-wear collections on the Paris catwalks, and before long his shows were a staple of the Paris openings.

The brilliance of the Italian workrooms continued to withstand comparison to the French ateliers. Quilted effects, lace insertions and embroideries gave depth to the collections, season after season.

As grandeur returned to fashion in the late 1970s after the confusion of the 1960s, ball gowns with ruched sleeves and big skirts made of multitudinous ruffled tiers recalled the great portraits of the eighteenth and nineteenth centuries. In a contrasting mood, narrow dresses with sheer inserts had a dramatic, modern air.

In the 1980s, Valentino's sense of luxury was given full rein and he was to be perceived as an exuberant leader in a new race for opulence. He was applauded also for his 'sense of self-renewal' (Pia Soli, in *Il Tempo*) and, underneath the obvious luxury of both shape and fabric, for his willingness to try inventive new cuts. He was, wrote Hebe Dorsey in the *International Herald Tribune*, able 'to serve a solid diet of sheer luxury while keeping it light and fun'.

meanwhile recognition grew and Valentino's work was widely praised. 'For the first time Paris took an Italian designer to its heart, with a kind of standing ovation usually reserved for the members of its own exclusive club,' Hebe Dorsey wrote in the *International Herald Tribune* in July 1982. 'It was long overdue, but Paris is tough on foreign competition and Italian designers are frankly hated.'

At home the Italians showed their appreciation of their native son. Valentino's drawings were included in an exhibition at the National Graphics Institute in Rome entitled 'The Design of Haute Couture from 1930 to 1970', an event that would have attracted little notice without his participation.

At the 25th anniversary of Valentino's couture house in Rome, in 1984, Renato Altissimo, Italy's Minister for Industry, presented the designer with a plaque honouring his contribution to fashion. The following year he was awarded his nation's Order of Merit by the Italian President, Sandra Pertini.

Valentino's presentations were not confined to Rome and Paris. At the invitation of Diana Vreeland he also showed his collection at the Metropolitan Museum of Art in New York. It was fitting, said Mrs Vreeland, who directed the museum's special fashion exhibitions for almost twenty years, that Valentino's work should be seen in an art museum. Other honours included an invitation to present his show in Tokyo at an event highlighting the best five designers in the world. He also received the keys to the city of Los Angeles after showing his clothes there.

t he 1980s closed with a triumphant show destined to become part of fashion history. It was based on motifs from the Wiener Werkstätte, an association of designers which flourished in Vienna in the early part of the twentieth century. Its dynamic geometric patterns were derived from furniture and architecture. The designs were bold and graphic, the most dramatic in black and white, with circles the size of dinner plates, and with broad stripes and bold squares. Valentino saw the Wiener Werkstätte designs as having a strong connection to the stark effects of the 1960s.

Almost a century after Josef Hoffmann worked in Vienna, his name became associated with fashion through Valentino's designs. Hoffmann's bold, austere modernism inspired designs of evening coats, strapless columns and jackets. His designs were also suggested in shoes, gloves and jewelry. It was a brave direction for fashion, where milder themes such as flowers usually predominated.

Valentino's work became increasingly mature during the 1980s, mixing elegant craftsmanship, luxurious but often delicate embroideries and complex pleating. Details carried echoes of diverse cultures, drawing on medieval statuary, eighteenth-century Chinese ceremonial screens, Japanese lacquered boxes and Art Deco architecture.

Wit often accompanied the transformation of design motifs from one medium to another. The bow of a diamond necklace was repeated in sequin-embroidered bows in three colours decorating the front of the jacket of a simple black suit. The tufting of the back of a nineteenth-century leather sofa was suggested by the quilting of an evening jacket embellished on its borders with embroidered flowers. The beaded surface of another jacket repeated the design of an American patchwork quilt. Most imaginatively, the rings to which horses were tethered in a sixteenth-century palace in Siena were transformed into braid and used as fastenings on a green velvet jacket.

Although the clothes exuded richness, the design often looked simple − soft crêpe pants worn with an embroidered bolero, for example, or a long chiffon skirt accompanied by an overblouse embroidered all over in sequins and mother-of-pearl beads (a design adapted from a sixteenth-century decorated footstool from India).

motifs favoured by Valentino from the beginning of his career were now being developed with even greater subtlety and sophistication. Pleats were used both horizontally and vertically to create patterns of their own. Animal patterns were achieved using fabrics alone, like the alternating black-and-white panels of pleated chiffon that slithered around the body to suggest a zebra's stripes.

Flesh-coloured chiffon is embroidered in gold, copper and brown sequins to resemble a leopard's spots, while in a long narrow dress under a black lace over-skirt the addition of black sequins gives the effect of a cobra's skin.

Not everything is severely classic. The double coat, for example, is a practical idea: two coats in matching or contrasting colours which can be buttoned together to form a single warm coat or separated to make two lighter garments. The colour combinations of these were a dark green coat over a purple one (shown with a purple jersey dress) and a mango and apricot coat over an apricot dress: a perfect combination for a weekend trip – and a wardrobe of manageable proportions. Such factors were not generally taken into account in couture collections.

On a less serious note there was the black knitted top embroidered in mother-of-pearl and beads. Pulled over a black satin skirt, this was reminiscent of the button-covered jacket which had been worn on stage by the British singer Boy George, and picked up by young, trendy Britons. It is a sign of Valentino's awareness of contemporary fashion trends, no matter how evanescent they may be, and a reminder that no designer can operate in a vacuum.

throughout his collections, there is an emphasis on black, often in combination with white or with beige tones, the colour of Devonshire cream. The black also serves as a background for what are often complex embroideries in metallic tones. This colour scheme, which provides a solid foundation for elegance in dress, is varied by Valentino's constant preoccupation with red. Red – whether chiffon, organza, satin or crêpe – has been a leitmotif throughout Valentino's career. It is a surefire attention-grabber, which helps to explain its popularity with film stars as well as with fashionable women who want to be noticed.

By the dawn of the 1990s, fashion had become truly global. Through the use of computers and rapidly transmitted photographs, a style introduced in Paris would be examined in Hong Kong almost instantaneously.

the Gulf War, in January 1991, was greeted with fear and apprehension all over the world, including the world of couture. After much anguish, most couturiers decided it would be better to proceed with the openings of their spring collections than to cancel them. Although most major countries sent press representatives to these shows, relatively large contingents from both Japan and the United States were missing. Many Europeans, whose journeys were shorter, managed to attend.

One of the positive elements of this season was Valentino's 'Peace' dress – a slender white crêpe column with the word 'Peace' embroidered horizontally in silver and grey beads in fourteen different languages. It was accompanied by a short white satin flaring coat with an appliquéd dove picked out in beads. Never had fashion so strongly expressed the spirit of the moment.

In June 1991, Valentino celebrated this thirtieth anniversary in Rome. More than three hundred styles were brought together for the show; more than five hundred guests attended the black-tie dinner. The women guests included world-class models, like Linda Evangelista, Claudia Schiffer and Dianne DeWitt, all devastatingly beautiful in Valentino gowns. Fellow couturiers Emanuel Ungaro, Hubert de Givenchy and Gianfranco Ferré paid homage to one of their own.

But the star of the evening was Elizabeth Taylor, who arrived late but radiant, in a shoulder-baring, bouffant Valentino dress.

The clothes – three decades of Valentino's designs – were grouped by theme, not chronologically. The effect was powerful, and the exhibition, which was repeated in 1992 in New York, where it attracted 70,000 visitors in two weeks, greatly enhanced Valentino's standing.

today, Valentino Garavani is a citizen of the world. In addition to the Rome-based couture operation, there are hundreds of shops selling his women's clothes all over the world, including Tokyo, Beirut and Seoul as well as Europe and the United States. His men's clothes are in hundreds of stores, similarly widely dispersed.

Valentino is responsible for four ready-to-wear collections a year and it is important to remember in this context that it is ready-to-wear which has extended the fashion audience and made fashion the truly global phenomenon it is today. Of course couture continues to be fashion's pathfinder, constantly narrowing the gap between fashion and art. But the role of the designer has grown to include the many who turn to ready-to-wear, as well as the few who can afford couture. Some rare designers, like Valentino, have managed to extend their role in the new order.

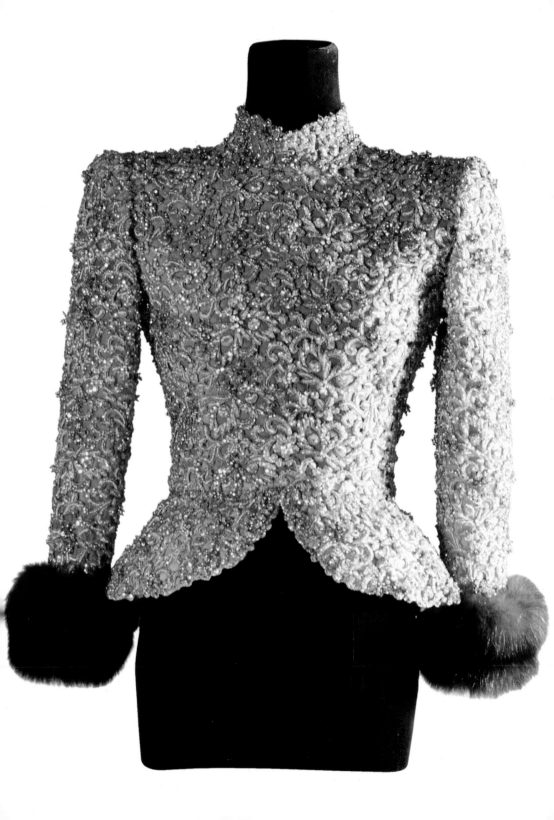

SPRING-SUMMER 59

AUTUMN-WINTER 62/63

AUTUMN-WINTER 63/64

SPRING-SUMMER 64

AUTUMN-WINTER 71/72

AUTUMN-WINTER 73/74

AUTUMN-WINTER 74/75

AUTUMN-WINTER 79/80

AUTUMN-WINTER 91/92

SPRING-SUMMER 92

SPRING-SUMMER 92

AUTUMN-WINTER 92/93

AUTUMN-WINTER 65/66   AUTUMN-WINTER 66/67   SPRING-SUMMER 68   SPRING-SUMMER 69

AUTUMN-WINTER 80/81   SPRING-SUMMER 82   AUTUMN-WINTER 88/89   AUTUMN-WINTER 89/90

SPRING-SUMMER 93   AUTUMN-WINTER 93/94   AUTUMN-WINTER 94/95   SPRING-SUMMER 95

Chronology

1932   Born in Voghera in Italy.

1959   Having completed his fashion studies and an apprenticeship with Jean Dessès and Guy Laroche, Valentino starts up his first studio in Rome.

1960   Begins his collaboration with Giancarlo Giammetti, who manages the commercial development of the House of Valentino.

1962   His first collection at the international fashion Gotha in the Palazzo Pitti, Florence, is a triumphant success.

1965   Valentino is recognized as the top name in Italian Haute Couture.

1967   He is awarded the Neiman Marcus Prize in Dallas (the equivalent of an Oscar in the world of fashion).

1968   Valentino's reputation is secured with the enormous success of his 'Collezione Bianca', the first clothes and accessories to have the magic 'V' label.
Opens a boutique in Avenue Montaigne, Paris.
Designs the wedding dress worn by Jacqueline Kennedy (a loyal client of Valentino's since 1964) for her marriage to Aristotle Onassis.

1969   Begins his Boutique line of clothes and opens the first Valentino shop in Milan.

1970   Launch of his first Ready-to-Wear collections.
Opening of Valentino boutiques in Rome and New York.
The first collection of accessories carrying his name comes on the market.

1971   Opening of the first menswear shop and home furnishing shop Valentino Più in Rome, both in Via Condotti.

1975   First fashion show of his Ready-to-Wear collection, in Paris.

1976   Opens a boutique in Tokyo.

1978   Launch of the Valentino Perfume at a gala evening in Paris, at the Théâtre des Champs Elysées.

1980   Opening of the first administrative offices in the United States and in Japan.

1982   Publication of the book *Valentino*, edited by Franco Maria Ricci.
20 September, Valentino presents his Autumn/Winter collection at the Metropolitan Museum in New York.

1984   Valentino celebrates his twenty-fifth year in the business and receives an official award from the Minister for Industry.

Opposite: Valentino Couture, Spring/Summer 1967.
Princess Luciana Pignatelli in black-and-white silk crêpe
pyjamas. Photo Henry Clarke. © ADAGP, Paris 1996.

Designs the kit for the Italian team in the Olympic Games in Los Angeles.

1985   He is awarded the Grand'Ufficiale dell'Ordine al Merito by the President of Italy.

1986   Receives the highest decoration possible in Italy, the Cavaliere di Gran Croce, from the President.

1988   Valentino fashion show at the Twentieth Century Fox studios in Hollywood.

1989   First show of the Haute Couture collection in Paris.

1990   In February, Valentino and Giancarlo Giammetti found L.I.F.E. (initials in Italian for 'Fighting, Informing, Building, Teaching'), an association working for the fight against AIDS.
The Accademia Valentino is officially opened to the public with an exhibition of painters of the Roman School.
Exhibition of 'The Art of Cartier' at the Accademia Valentino. Publication of the book *Valentino: Trent'Anni de Magia*, by Leonardo.

1991   To celebrate his thirtieth year in the fashion business, an exhibition entitled 'Valentino: Thirty Years of Magic' is organized in Valentino's honour by the Mayor of Rome at the Capitoline Museum, while the Accademia Valentino presents a retrospective of his designs.
Creation of the perfume 'Vendetta', for men and women.

1992   Exhibition at the Accademia Valentino entitled: 'La seduzione da Boucher a Warhol'.
The 'Valentino: Thirty Years of Magic' exhibition is invited to go to New York to coincide with the fifth centenary celebrations of the discovery of America. Over 70,000 people visit the show in less than two weeks.

1993   Valentino is invited by the Chinese government to stage a show in Beijing.

1994   In January, Valentino presents his first ever costume designs at the Eisenhower Theatre in the John Fitzgerald Kennedy Centre, Washington, for an opera entitled *The Dream of Valentino*, based on the life of the movie star Rudolf Valentino.

1995   Valentino's return to Italy is celebrated on 14 January in Florence with a fashion show at the Stazione Leopolda, over thirty years after his first show at the Palazzo Pitti. The Mayor of Florence awards him the 'Premio speciale dell'arte nella moda'. Exhibition of archeology at the Accademia Valentino entitled: 'I misteri di una fanciulla'.

1996   Exhibition at the Accademia Valentino of Leonardo da Vinci's work entitled 'Il codice Leicester'. Valentino is named Cavaliere de Lavoro.

Chronology and captions translated by Saron Hughes

Opposite: The inseparable trio: Valentino, Rome and La Dolce Vita. Evening dress, Valentino Night, Spring/Summer 1995, trailing in the Trevi fountain in Rome. Photo © Arthur Elgort.

Valentino

Empire-line dress. Valentino Couture Autumn/Winter 1965–66. Red strapless dress in silk crêpe, with straight neckline and cleft at the front. This dress was modelled by Princess Luciana Pignatelli at a show in New York in front of an audience composed entirely of European aristocrats. Photo © Janos Grapow.
Luxury and refinement. Valentino Couture Autumn/Winter 1969–1970. Cape in triple-layered black silk organza, worn by Audrey Hepburn. Photo © Gian Paolo Barbieri.

Valentino's poppy red. 'Red is a fascinating colour; the colour of life, blood and death, passion and love; the ultimate cure for sadness' (Valentino). Evening dresses, Valentino Couture. From left to right: Autumn/Winter 1989, with draped sleeve in the shape of a petal; Autumn/Winter 1984–85, with vertical drapery; Autumn/Winter 1987–88, with looped ribbon decoration; Autumn/Winter 1989–90, with symmetrical drapery; Spring/Summer 1985, caught up at the back for a closer fit with two bow accents; Spring/Summer 1983, in pleated fabric with fringes. Photo © Janos Grapow.

Valentino in his studio in Rome, 54 Via Gregoriana, in the early 1960s. The couturier's fascination with the colour red can already be seen in the décor. Photo © TEAM/Grazia Neri.

Valentino's animal prints. Valentino Couture Spring/Summer 1966. Caftan in white cotton satin with black giraffe print, worn by Donyale Luna over hooded white silk pyjamas. Photo © Marc Hispard.
Prints in Rome. Valentino Couture Spring/Summer 1966. Cotton satin pyjamas with black-and-white giraffe print, worn by Mirella Petteni. Behind her is the Trevi Fountain in Rome, symbolic of the designer's Roman identity. Photo Henry Clarke. © ADAGP, Paris 1996.

The bold graphic. Valentino Couture Spring/Summer 1967. On the roof tops of Rome, Veruschka wears a caftan in silk ottoman over chiffon pyjamas. Photo © Franco Rubartelli, 1967. *Vogue Italia*, Edizioni Condé Nast/Grazia Neri.
The uncompromising line. Valentino Couture Spring/Summer 1996. Inspired by the geometrical drawings of the Wiener Werkstätte, Valentino uses the sobriety of black and white in his collections as a counterpoint to all the colour. Photo © Patrick Demarchelier.

Animal influence. 'Animal print' fabrics are among Valentino's favourites and he often used them in his designs in the 1960s for dressing the stars. Left-hand page: In Trastevere in Rome, Veruschka wears a coat and trouser suit in tiger print wool. Photo © Franco Rubartelli. Right-hand page: left: Valentino Couture Autumn/Winter 1966–67, leopard print jacket and trouser suit in wool. On the right: Valentino Couture Spring/Summer 1967 © Janos Grapow.

The Arabian influence. Valentino Couture Spring/Summer 1976. Pearly grey satin tunic with pinkish beige beads, embroidered in patterns based on mosque mosaics. Photo © Janos Grapow.

The purity of white. Valentino Couture Spring/Summer 1968. Dressed in Valentino's lucky colour, Benedetta Barzini and Marisa Berenson wear cotton dress suits embroidered in beads and strass. Photo Henry Clarke. Courtesy of *Vogue* USA © 1968 Condé Nast Publications Inc. © ADAGP, Paris 1996.

Inspired by the Incas. Valentino Couture Spring/Summer 1966. Donyale Luna wears a silk caftan over chiffon pyjamas. This ethnic-looking outfit, inspired by the Aztec calendar, is made of fabric printed in warm yellows, reds and rust colours. Photo © Marc Hispard.

A change of scenery with a change of colour. Valentino Couture Spring/Summer 1967. Mirella Petteni wears a pink and yellow woollen ensemble. Photo © Gian Paolo Barbieri.

Valentino in his studio in Rome, in the early 1960s. The dressmaker's dummy still provides the basic shape for Valentino's designs. Photo © TEAM/Grazia Neri.

A homage to flowers. Valentino Couture Spring/Summer 1972. Angelica Huston is swathed in a yellow silk organza dress printed with large pink lotus flowers. Photo © Gian Paolo Barbieri.

Luxury and sophistication. Valentino Couture Spring/Summer 1969. Veruschka wears an orange satin silk poncho decorated with a long fringe and a belt made from coral beads. Worn by Princess Grace with white organza trousers at the Bal de la Rose in Monaco. Photo © Franco Rubartelli.

Rome. Valentino with Aly Dunne at the Mignanelli Palace in Rome, 1989. Aly Dunne wears a full-length dress from the Spring/Summer Couture Collection 1989. Photo © Barry McKinley.

Sculptural drapery. Valentino Couture Spring/Summer 1981. Full-length red organza dress with spiralling drapery, modelled by Brooke Shields at the age of fifteen for a fashion show in Rome. Photo © Janos Grapow.

Woman in Valentino dress by Fernando Botero. Oil on canvas. Valentino has always found a wealth of ideas in the world of fine art and is a dedicated collector. In return, Fernando Botero pays homage to the couturier and to the timeless Valentino red. Rome, Collection of Valentino Garavani. Photo © Valentino Archive.

Jackie Kennedy in Cambodia, 1967. Valentino Couture Autumn/Winter 1966–67. Aquamarine toga-style satin dress, edged with silver and rhinestone embroidery. Worn here by Jacqueline Kennedy for an official visit, for which Valentino designed her entire wardrobe. Photo © Scheler/Stern (right). Photo © Janos Grapow (left).

The Bow. Valentino Ready-to-Wear Autumn/Winter 1988–89. Black heavy satin evening dress with three white bows. For Valentino, 'Bows are an obvious symbol of total femininity. They are absolutely indispensable . . . an elegant finishing touch to complement a swirl of drapery.' Photo © Walter Chin.

The Flower. Valentino Couture Spring/Summer 1969. Audrey Hepburn wears a cape in white triple-layered silk organza in the shape of rose petals. Photo © Gian Paolo Barbieri.

The 'Shadow' Collection. Valentino Couture Autumn/Winter 1979–80. Brown woollen suit buttoned at the back with a shadow effect below the jacket. In this 'Shadow' collection, strips of velvet are added to look like openings in some designs, while in others, taffeta and chiffon suggest cuffs, collars and hems. Photo © Janos Grapow.

Fakes. Valentino Couture Autumn/Winter 1987–88. Zebra-effect sleeveless top in gathered chiffon. ' . . . due to modern day processes, the massacre of animals can now be avoided, so why go on killing? . . . . Even by 1962, I had invented fake black zebra skin' (Valentino). Photo © Janos Grapow.
Turn-of-the-century traditional Russian costume. Valentino Couture Autumn/Winter 1986–87. Beige chiffon jacket embroidered with gold braid, rhinestones, small beads and golden sequins to give a macramé effect. Photo © Janos Grapow.

The Sublime. Valentino Couture Autumn/Winter 1986–87. Red neo-classical silk crêpe-dress. The shoulder straps join at the back and extend down to form the source of the drape. Photo © Noëlle Hoeppe.
Precision and elegance. Valentino Couture Autumn/Winter 1989–90. Black-and-white satin evening dress with decorative pattern inspired by the work of Josef Hoffmann, whom Valentino considers to be the master of precision. Photo © Cristina Ghergo.

The Hoffmann influence. Valentino Couture Autumn/Winter 1989–90. Long pareo-style dress in draped black silk worn with a long white satin coat embroidered with black beads. The entire collection is inspired by the work of the Austrian architect and interior designer Josef Hoffmann who worked in Vienna at the beginning of the twentieth century. Photo © Walter Chin. On the right is a sketch for the same outfit. © Valentino Archive.

Valentino's sketches. Some designs from Valentino Couture collections from the beginning to those of today. Femininity and elegance remain the essential criteria for his creations. © Valentino Archive.

The famous 'White' collection. Valentino Couture Spring/Summer 1968. Worn by Marisa Berenson, this short organza dress with embroidered flowers and pleated flounce cuffs belonged to Audrey Hepburn. Photo Henry Clarke. © ADAGP, Paris, 1996.
The 'Orchid' collection. Valentino Couture Autumn/Winter 1995–96. Black dress decorated with orchids, made of embroidered lace over tulle, with asymmetrical neckline and overskirt in black faille lined with pink satin; worn here by Naomi Campbell. Photo © Walter Chin.

The Grand Hotel, Paris. Valentino Couture Autumn/Winter 1994–95. A collection of evening dresses. From left to right: pink taffeta puff ball dress edged with embroidered black lace; black embroidered chiffon dress with horizontal strips; silver dress with grey taffeta skirt and embroidered black tulle top; black chiffon dress; silver panne velvet dress with lace insets and top made entirely of lace; honey-coloured satin Empire-line dress. Photo © Arthur Elgort.

Cheeky pink. Valentino Couture Autumn/Winter 1990–91. Sketch by Mats Gustafson for a pink woollen coat. © Mats Gustafson, A+C Anthology.
Exotic pink. Valentino Couture Autumn/Winter 1995–96. Naomi Campbell wears a mauve full-length velvet and satin silk dress with insets placed on the diagonal. The straps are made of embroidered orchids, which were the inspiration for the entire collection. Photo © Walter Chin.

Simply 'Divine'. Valentino Couture Autumn/Winter 1965-66. Veruschka wears the famous Empire-line dress with a long red tulle coat made entirely from embroidered ostrich feathers. Photo © Henry Clarke. Courtesy of *Vogue* USA © 1968 Condé Nast Publications Inc. © ADAGP, Paris 1996.
Sweet sophistication. Valentino Boutique Spring/Summer 1996. Evening dresses, from left to right: in pink crêpe and satin silk; in beige crêpe and satin silk, embroidered on the back with flowers, and in green crêpe and silk. Photo © Patrick Demarchelier.

Valentino and his models, after his 1992 Spring/Summer Couture fashion show. From left to right: Claudia Schiffer in a full-length black tulle dress embroidered with white flowers; Beverly Peele in black and white; Nadège; Yasmeen Ghaury in a long dress with diagonal stripes, and Karen Mulder in a long black-and-white *point d'esprit* dress. Photo © Roxanne Lowit.

Timeless modernity. Left: Valentino Boutique Spring/Summer 1996–97. Cocktail outfit made of burgundy, olive and navy blue chiffon with inlays and braid embroidery. Photo © Max Colin. Right: Valentino Couture Spring/Summer 1996. Full-length black dress in satin organza caught up at the back, with slip in embroidered lace. Photo © Walter Chin.

Rome in the feminine. Valentino Boutique Spring/Summer 1995. This photograph, taken in the Piazza del Campidoglio for the 'Dolce Vita' publicity campaign, shows Claudia Schiffer wearing a wool and silk suit in blue and off-white. Photo © Arthur Elgort.

'La Dolce Vita'. Valentino Boutique Spring/Summer 1995. This photograph was taken by Arthur Elgort for the 'Dolce Vita' publicity campaign. Claudia Schiffer poses, surrounded by seamstresses, in one of the Haute Couture workshops in the Valentino studio in Rome wearing a dress in tartan taffeta and an overskirt with lace inlay. Photo © Arthur Elgort.

An evening at the Opera. Designed by Valentino in 1953, this dress was not made until 1991 for the exhibition 'Valentino: Thirty Years of Magic' in Rome. It was one of the 'Dream' designs in which his favourite themes – the use of black, white and drapery – were already apparent. Photo © Valentino Archive.
The design finally realized. Worn here by Christy Turlington, the white satin sheath dress with black embroidery and train made of black silk taffeta in the form of a panel. Photo © Steven Meisel, A+C Anthology. *Vogue Italia*, March 1986.

Acknowledgments

The publisher would like to thank the house of Valentino for their help in the realization of this work and in particular Carlos de Souza, Violante Valdettaro and Olivia Berghauer.

Thanks also to Fernando Botero, Angelica Huston, Marisa Berenson and Princess Luciana Pignatelli.

To Arthur Elgort, Henry Clarke, Walter Chin, Janos Grapow, Gian Paolo Barbieri, Marc Hispard, Max Colin, Noëlle Hoeppe, Franco Rubartelli, Mr Tyen, Patrick Demarchelier, Grazia Neri, Steven Meisel, Mats Gustafson, Cristina Ghergo, Roxanne Lowit.

Also to Helena Christensen, Claudia Schiffer, Christy Turlington, Naomi Campbell, Stella Tennant, Veruschka, Donyale Luna, Aly Dunne, Trish Goff, Kirsty Hume, Nadège, Beverly Peele, Mirella Petteni, Benedetta Barzini, Yasmeen Ghaury, Karen Mulder, Nadja Auermann, Carla Bruni, Kalina, Giorgina.

Finally, this book would have been impossible without the help of Auro Varani, Sandrine Bleu, Gwenaëlle Dautricourt (*Marie Claire*), Gino (Agence TEAM), Mimi Brown (Art & Commerce), Michelle, Matthew Godrich (Marek & Associates), Nicole Chamson (ADAGP), Susan Geller (Susan Geller & Associates), Bryan Bantry and Angela, also Sabine Killinger (Elite), Jean-Marc (Marilyn Agency), Cathy Queen (Ford NY), Chantal Fagnou (VIVA) and Aline Souliers-Lorale (Metropolitan).

We hope they will accept this expression of our sincere gratitude.